THE BEGINNINGS OF BEDFORD

David Baker and Evelyn Baker

Illustrations by Andrew Pinder and Evelyn Baker

BEDFORDSHIRE COUNTY PLANNING DEPARTMENT

CONTENTS

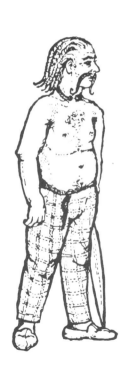

5000 BC
Stone Age

1500 BC
Bronze Age

500 BC
Iron Age

AD 200
Roman

AD 850
Saxon

AD 1070
Norman

12th century   13th century   14th century   15th century   late 15th century   16th century

1 Looking at Early Bedford

Imagine climbing the tower of St Paul's Church in 1610 and looking out over Bedford. During the last ten years King James I has succeeded the first Queen Elizabeth and survived the Gunpowder Plot. Your modern eyes expect to see a town, but find an overgrown village. Fields lie in place of the Bus Station, De Parys Avenue, Castle Road and County Hall. The buildings are quaint and small, though they line a familiar pattern of streets.

We know this from John Speed's map, printed in 1610, and our earliest picture of the town. It is a vital link between past and present. We can recognise his plan of streets, yet what he drew had already existed for seven hundred years.

Exploring these early centuries is like hunting by candlelight for the lost pieces of a jigsaw. Surviving historical documents are scarce: not many people could write or read in 1610, and even fewer before 1200. There are only two medieval buildings left in modern Bedford other than churches; St John's Hospital is opposite Telephone House and fragments of the George Inn are tucked behind Debenhams in the High Street. Since 1967, archaeology has begun to discover the buried remains of vanished Bedford, but over 50 rescue excavations have probed only a small part of the historic core. A few clues can be seen above ground in the present day town.

This book explores the beginnings of Bedford, up to the time of John Speed's map. What was here before the town? When was Bedford founded, and who laid out the regular street plan? What was the effect of the Norman castle and its sieges? How did Saxon and medieval Bedfordians live? Some of the answers are guesswork based on what we know of the historical period. Others rely upon reconstructing a picture from the incomplete jigsaw available to us now. When more pieces are found we may have to change our ideas about the overall pattern they make.

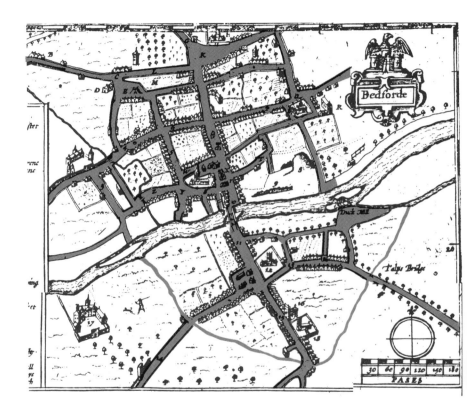

John Speed's map of Bedford was part of a larger map of Bedfordshire, published in 1610. This used the 16th century work of Christopher Saxton, but the inset of Bedford in the upper right-hand corner seems to have been Speed's own work. He shows each building very clearly, and must have surveyed the street plan. Some of his detail may be inaccurate or incomplete, but historians think what he shows of Bedford is fairly true to what he saw.

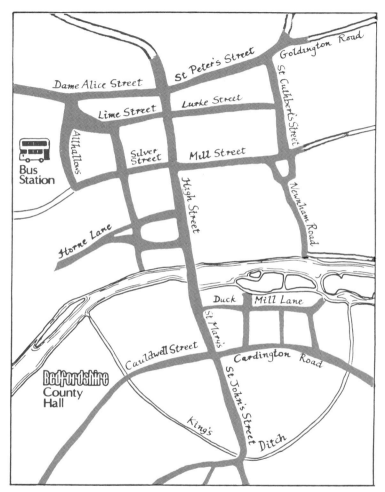

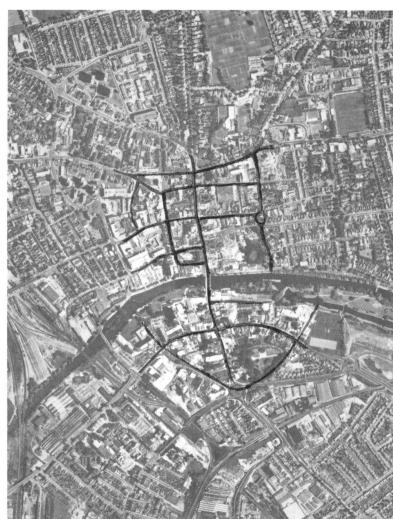

These three plans help you to see early Bedford within the modern town. On the left is our oldest map, showing Bedford in 1610; on the right is a recent aerial photograph. The sketch above shows the streets coloured on both plans.

2 Before the Town of Bedford

Beda's ford

Stone Age axes, Roman coin and early Saxon pottery

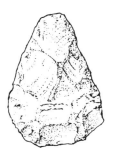   

Prehistoric farmers were attracted to the broad river valley of the Ouse (which means 'river') long before there was a town. The well-drained fertile soils were easily cleared of vegetation and light to plough. Stone Age tools, as well as tools and pottery from the Bronze and Iron Ages, have been found in the modern fields. During the last ten years, archaeologists have excavated Iron Age and Roman peasant farmsteads near Odell, Radwell, Bromham, Newnham and Willington.

The early Saxon migrants from the continent also mostly lived in scattered farmsteads rather than the modern villages we know today. Some were buried in the cemetery which was discovered on the site of Kempston's Saxon Centre in the 1860s. Kempston may have been the most important local settlement at this time. Early Saxon pottery dug up in Horne Lane probably marks a group of dwellings by a river ford. It may have been the home of a long-forgotten Saxon called Beda, so famous in his day that his name became the place – Bedford means Beda's Ford.

The villages of the Ouse valley came into being between 700 and 1200. The Domesday Survey of 1086 records people living in Cardington, Kempston, Elstow, Biddenham, Bromham, Stagsden, Oakley, Pavenham, Milton Ernest and Radwell. But by then Bedford was already a town; how did this happen?

The river crossing at Beda's Ford was important for local communications and trade; settlers were drawn to it. More and more people came to live on the north bank. Eventually the settlement became a town. At some time, a grid of streets running at right angles to each other was deliberately laid out. The resulting plan was markedly different from an irregular layout growing slowly over the centuries.

When did this happen? There is no definite evidence, but it must have been sometime during the Saxon period. The town was here in 1066 when the Normans carefully sited their castle to dominate an existing Saxon street plan. Our search for the date of this planning must first explore Saxon history for occasions when this might have happened, and then match the possibilities with what we know of Bedford itself.

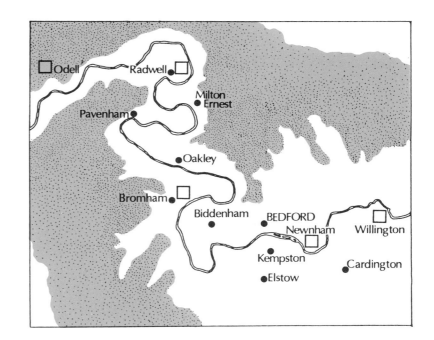

The valley of the meandering Ouse broadens at Bedford. The squares on this map show where Iron Age and Roman peasant farmsteads have been excavated: others probably existed also. The dots between Radwell and Cardington show places recorded in Domesday Book, though not necessarily in their modern positions.

3 Bedford in Saxon England

More than six centuries passed between the end of Roman influence about 410 and the arrival of William the Conqueror in 1066. The years between 410 and 700 have been called the Dark Ages because so little is known about them. In 400, Britannia was the northern-most province of the fading Roman Empire. During the next century the land was overrun by tribes of Angles and Saxons moving in from the continent. By 700 these had grouped together into a number of kingdoms. Their rivalries were complicated by a series of Danish and Norwegian Viking invasions from 835 until the early 11th century. What part did the Bedford area play in the history of Saxon England?

The Migration

Saxon raiders and settlers had been crossing the North Sea for decades by the time Britain's links with Rome were finally cut. The newcomers found the native British living in a tribal society much like their own, little changed from Iron Age times before the Romans came. The towns, roads and villas introduced by the Romans were mostly abandoned within a few generations. Many local inhabitants were driven from their lands, but not without a struggle. One battle the native British fought (and lost) was against the West Saxon leader Cuthwulf in 571 at a place called *Biedcanford*. The name sounds similar, but this almost certainly was not Bedford. Overall, che English population seems to have dwindled during the 6th and 7th centuries, even with extra people coming in from the continent. The reason may have been plague and food shortages caused by a worsening climate rather than fighting.

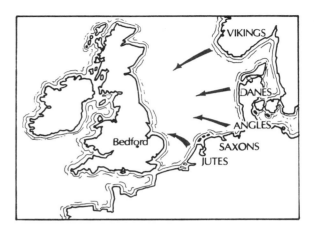

Immigrants and Invaders, 400-1000

Mercia and the areas under Mercian influence, *c.*790

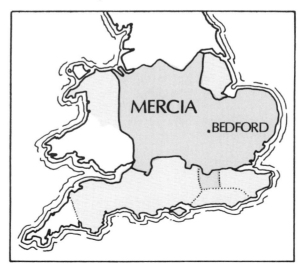

Coin of King Offa (*d.*796). It reads: OFFA · REX with a cross before and after. The portrait is taken from a Roman coin rather than from life.

Middle Saxon Kingdoms

By about 700, the early migrations were over, and peace was returning to England. Peoples and tribes were grouping together in kingdoms. The population was growing; some abandoned towns were lived in again. Trade increased and stimulated the foundation of other trading centres. Christianity spread, driving out the pagan gods, and Bedford seems to have been a missionary base for its area.

After the 750s, Mercia became the most powerful kingdom south of the river Humber. King Offa was the strongest ruler in England since the Romans, and renowned throughout Europe. He created towns in order to improve trade and defence. In the 780s and 790s raiders from Scandinavia began to threaten south-east England. Offa may have sought to defend his subjects by fortifying a chain of towns along the southern and eastern borders of his kingdom. Beda's Ford, perhaps already a royal centre, may have become one vital link in that chain.

Raiders from the North

Offa died in 796. The medieval chronicler Matthew Paris, writing many years later, recorded a tradition that he was buried in Bedford, but there is no other evidence for this. After his death, the southern kingdom of Wessex began to grow at Mercia's expense; however, regular Scandinavian invasions began in 835. By 850 the Danes were staying all winter in England instead of concentrating upon brief summer raids from bases in their homelands. In 865 a great army invaded East Anglia, intent on conquering and settling land. The Wessex kings resisted without much success.

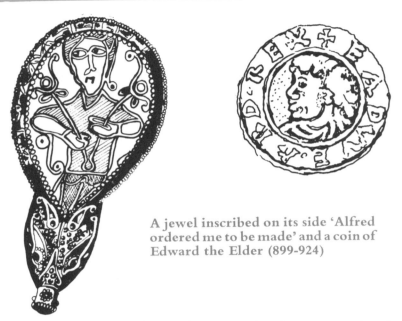

A jewel inscribed on its side 'Alfred ordered me to be made' and a coin of Edward the Elder (899-924)

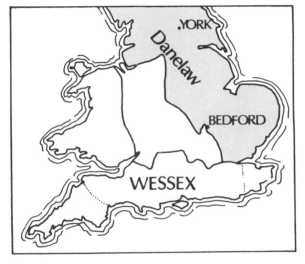

The Danelaw boundary in 886

Alfred of Wessex became king in 871, but the Danes continued to gain ground. They drove him back to Athelney in the marshes of Somerset, where legend tells us he burnt those famous cakes. Then Alfred fought back; in 886 he forced a treaty and Christian baptism upon the Danish leader Guthrum. In the Bedfordshire region, the treaty boundary between Wessex and the Danelaw land ran

up the Thames, and then up the Lea, and along the Lea to its source, and then in a straight line to Bedford, and then up the Ouse to Watling Street.

After Alfred's death in 899, the Danes moved again. They occupied Bedford as a centre for their lands to the south and west. Alfred's son Edward the Elder continued his father's fight. His successful military campaigns pushed forward the frontiers of Wessex northwards. He took control of land occupied by the Danish settlers. Key towns (called 'burhs' or boroughs) were captured and strengthened. They dominated each newly won area and provided a springboard for the next conquest.

Bedford Recaptured

In 914 Edward built a burh at Buckingham. As a result, the Danish leader

Earl Thurcetel came and accepted him as his lord, and so did all the earls and principal men who belonged to Bedford.

Clearly Bedford .was an important place by this time, and the township on the north bank of the river was probably already fortified. In 915 Edward

went with his army to Bedford before Martinmas and obtained the borough . . . and he stayed there four weeks, and before he went away he ordered the borough on the south side of the river to be built.

The Danes Again

Peace did not last for long: the Danes counter-attacked. Two years later they set up a camp near Tempsford.

And they went until they reached Bedford; and the men who were inside went out against them and fought against them, and put them to flight and killed a good part of them.

Later that year this same Danish force was decisively defeated, and the Danes settled down as part of the local population.

Even this was not the end of Scandinavian troubles. Further invasions by better organised armies began in the 980s. The English ruler Aethelred the Unready had no military answer. Bedford suffered in 1009-1010, when the Danes came from the north

along the Ouse until they reached Bedford and so on as far as Tempsford, and ever they burnt as they went.

Afterwards, on Aethelred's death in 1016, the Danish ruler Cnut took the English throne, restoring order and peace. The next major invasion came from nearer at hand: it was the Norman Conquest of 1066.

These quotations come from the *Anglo-Saxon Chronicle,* one of the most important sources for early English history. Several copies taken from a 9th century compilation were continued at a number of centres, the latest until the mid 12th century.

King Cnut, from manuscript of *c.*1031

4 Who was Bedford's first Town Planner?

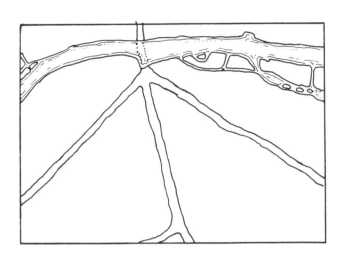

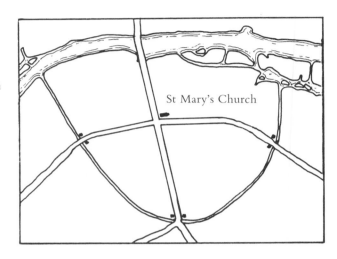

St Mary's Church

Bedford south of the Ouse:
left **tracks converge on the ford before 915**
right **the fortified borough after 915**

At some time in the Saxon period Bedford was organised and planned as a town. By the 780s or 790s Bedford may have become an important place for both King Offa and the Christian church. The main approach to the river crossing, down what is now High Street, may have had the earliest church of St Paul on one side and possibly some royal centre, including a small palace, in what is now the Castle Lane area. This settlement needed defences against recurring threats of attack. When were these provided, and who did it?

Were the Danes responsible? They had occupied the town for 25 years before Edward the Elder took it in 915. They are unlikely candidates because Danish conquerors preferred using other people's ready-made defences rather than creating their own. The time immediately after the Danish raid of 1009-10, which burnt the town, is equally unlikely. Flimsy wooden houses could easily be rebuilt on the existing network of streets if there was no reason to change it.

South Bedford

The origins of the town south of the river are easier to find. As we have seen, the Anglo-Saxon Chronicle tells us that during his visit in 915-916 Edward the Elder ordered a burh to be built. This must be the D-shaped enclosure outlined by the King's Ditch. It was a ditch dug for defence, and had a bank on the inside which also acted as a flood barrier. These new defences were to decide the layout of medieval and modern Bedford south of the river.

Any houses already standing south of the Ouse were probably near where three main routes met at the ford or bridge. The approach to the river must have been changed by the new defences. As the western route (now Cauldwell Street) and the eastern (now Cardington Road) crossed the new bank and ditch, they were turned slightly southwards towards each other instead of continuing up to the river. They met in the centre of the new burh at cross-roads with the old route (now St Mary's and St John's Streets) coming in from the south. This cross-pattern helped defenders to move rapidly around the whole defended area, and protect both river crossing and gates.

The parish of St Mary's was probably created at this time; it may have been carved out of the older parishes of Kempston and Elstow if they had originally come right up to the river. Edward may even at that time have provided its inhabitants with a new church at the cross-roads. Traces of late Saxon houses have been excavated on both sides of St John's Street.

Reconstruction of the King's Ditch: the bank has a timber defence and there is a path around the base between it and the Ditch: these can also be seen in cross-section

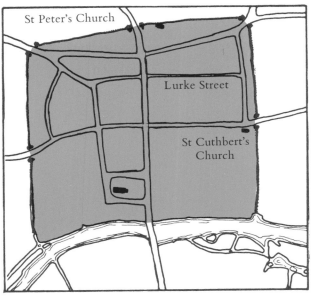

Bedford north of the Ouse, possible early urban limits:
left the Edward the Elder theory, *c.*915
right the Offa theory, *c.*795

North Bedford – Edward the Elder?

But did King Edward also plan the grid of streets north of the river, as one historian has suggested? He thought Edward would have treated Bedford in the same way Alfred and his successors treated Wessex towns further south. What would this have meant for the boundaries of Bedford?

This idea placed the western boundary of the town along the line of the Saffron Ditch and All Hallows running up to St Loye's. The northern boundary included the late Saxon church of St Peter as part of the defences. Its tower and stone walls acted as a bastion or strong point for a gateway. The eastern boundary ran down St Cuthbert's Street, and St Cuthbert's Church was also part of the defences. The line continued south to the river, on the original straight course of Newnham Street before it was forced to curve slightly outwards round the castle mound. The main difficulty with this theory is that the Anglo-Saxon Chronicle tells us Bedford was already fortified in 915.

North Bedford – King Offa?

Another historian has tried to solve this problem by looking for still earlier possibilities. He considered the 780s or 790s a more likely time, and thinks that King Offa would have treated Bedford like the other towns he had fortified further north in Mercia.

He thinks that the original burh was smaller. The best clues to its limits are the early parish boundaries of St Paul's, and some features that can still be seen in the layout of Bedford today. The northern limit was marked by St Paul's parish boundary which ran along Lime and Lurke Streets. Where these two streets met with the High Street was also the original meeting point for routes coming into the town. Look along High Street and you can see a clear change in ground slope here, and this may be significant. St Peter's Church was not built for at least another century, and then to serve the small settlement growing up around the green, north of the main east-west route past Bedford, now represented by Dame Alice Street and St Peter's Street.

The old parish boundary of St Paul turned south three-quarters of the way along Lurke Street on the eastern limit of the burh. South of Mill Street the parish boundary now wavers eastwards, forced out by the placing of the 11th century castle mound directly over it. St Cuthbert's Church, like St Peter's, is a later foundation serving a small settlement outside the original eastern defences.

The river was a natural southern limit, but the western one is more difficult to find. It may have run across Midland Road just east of a bend that can still be seen amid the shopping crowds. That bend is about the same distance *westwards* from High Street as the opposite boundary of St Paul's parish is *eastwards* from High Street. All Hallows Lane may be a later road created by people and carts needing a way round outside the line of the defences. All Saints Church which used to stand here may have served another later settlement outside the defences, like St Peter's and St Cuthbert's.

Hints of old boundaries: *above* the curve in Midland Road *below* the High Street bump near Lime Street

Who planned Bedford?

Both arguments agree that the land within this defended rectangle was divided into squares by streets: many of these exist today. It was an economic, fair and efficient division of land – modern New York is laid out on the same principle. The High Street ran straight down towards the bridge, following its ancient route and providing the central spine off which the side roads came.

Which idea is right? We may not be sure of the answer for a long time, if ever. One of the major problems is that no traces of defences have yet been found north of the river. These could easily have been destroyed by later expansion of the town. We know more about Edward's times than about Offa's, but the idea of an early small defended area with later suburbs growing outside seems more likely. Probably both rulers had a hand in creating the town the Normans found in 1066, Offa mainly in the north, Edward in the south.

5 How the Saxons lived in Bedford

How did the people of Bedford live in these early times? The further back in time we need to go, the fewer clues we have. For Middle Saxon times, about 1,200 years ago, we have to rely almost entirely upon archaeology.

Middle Saxon Houses

Excavations in the area later occupied by the castle have revealed stains in the earth which were all that remained of timber houses. Saxons lived here long enough to need to rebuild their houses several times. The plans of these dwellings, and more complete ones found in other places, allow archaeologists to work out how they were constructed. They were quite large, the size of a small bungalow, and probably fairly comfortable. The house frame was made of wood; draughts were kept out by slapping on a layer of clay mixed with animal dung, chopped straw and animal hair over the wattle walls. They had beaten earth floors, and roofs thickly covered with thatch to keep in the warmth. There were no clay roof-tiles at this time; that skill had been lost since the end of the Roman period. By our standards life was primitive: food was cooked on a hearth in the middle of the room; the smoke wafted up and eventually out of a hole in the roof. Toilet arrangements were simply a hole in the ground.

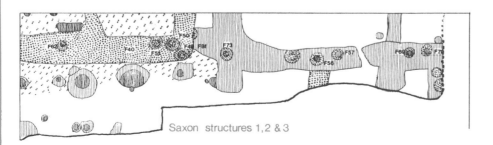

Saxon structures 1, 2 & 3

Left above: **a reconstruction of a typical Middle Saxon house**
below: **plan of earth stains representing foundations of successive timber houses excavated south of Castle Lane**

Pots, Tools and Rubbish

Archaeologists find only a few possessions from this time, because they cannot survive centuries in the ground. Wood, cloth or leather decays if not preserved in special conditions. Metal was precious and often melted down for re-use when broken or worn. The most frequent finds are animal bones and pottery.

Many useful tools were made from bone, a fairly soft material that was often richly decorated by carving. This comb made of antler was found in one of the houses. By studying the bones found on archaeological sites we can tell a great deal about the people who threw them away. What sort of animals were they rearing? Which meat did they prefer? How old were the animals when slaughtered? How did butchers cut the meat? Did some households have choicer cuts than others? What diseases did the animals have? How did people use the bones?

In a time before tins, plastic cartons and clingfilm, everyday containers were made of pottery, wood, and even leather. Metals were expensive, so most cooking had to be done in pottery containers. Being made of clay and rather brittle, they often broke and were discarded, only to be rediscovered and studied centuries later.

Pottery is probably the most useful type of rubbish of all for telling us about its owners. The Saxon pottery in these houses was probably handmade by local people and fired in a simple bonfire kiln. The shape of vessels and the marks on them show us the cooking or storage methods, whether they were simmering in a metal couldron, catching drips from roasting meat or sitting in the fire. Pots can tell us whether they belonged to wealthy households importing costly vessels, humble homes or industry. Sometimes traces of food have survived for analysis by scientists today.

We need to find and dig more of these Middle Saxon houses together with their rubbish pits in order to find out more about these earliest Bedfordians. At the moment we have no way of knowing whether they represent scattered dwellings by the ford or part of a more organised settlement.

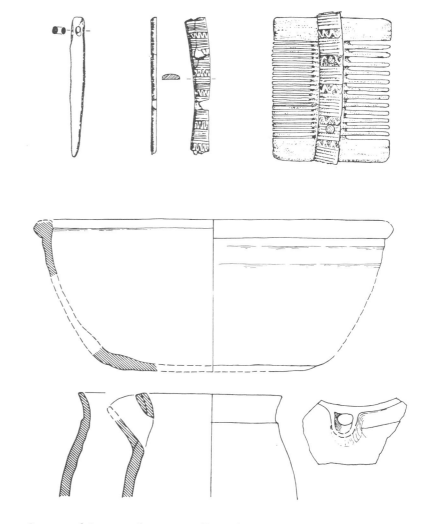

Saxon objects: a bone needle, a bone comb (and reconstruction) a bowl and a spouted pitcher

17

By the 10th century, Bedford was already a flourishing market town, attracting a wide range of commercial activities. Though still tiny by modern standards, it was nevertheless a major centre in the region. Its importance is shown by the fact that it minted silver coins for the king. Documents record five moneyers working here. Making coins was a fairly simple process, and the mints will have left no traces, unless the archaeologists find the coin dies or trial pieces discovered elsewhere. Many of the coins can be seen in Bedford and Luton museums.

Reconstruction of later Saxon house

Later Saxon Life

In the later Saxon period, especially after Edward the Elder's foundation of the southern town in 915-16, there seem to have been more people occupying a larger area of land. They too lived in wooden houses with thatched or wood roofs. Many traces of their homes have been found underlying the present town, the most complete ones along the edge of St John's Street and Midland Road. They also put much of their household rubbish in pits near their houses and this has told us much about the way they lived. Earth samples were taken from a cess pit (or lavatory pit) found under the new Bedford Museum. Close examination by scientists revealed the remains of plants and insects alive at the time: other rubbish included many different kinds of bird, fish and animal bones, as well as seeds and fruit stones, the remnants of long-ago meals. The pits were crawling with millipedes when in use.

Striking coins on a portable mint

Of course the Danes must also have made an impact on the town. Many of them must have settled and married with the native people: we find Danish names like Baldwin in 10th century Bedford. Three moneyers at the mint also had Danish names, Grim, Gunni and Ulcetel. The extent of the inter-mingling is shown by the difficulty archaeologists have in telling the difference between Danish and Saxon activity from the tools and rubbish they left behind.

These people left many different types of pottery. This shows that Bedfordians by this time were trading in goods coming from quite long distances. We can recognise distinctive types of pot which were made in Stamford and on the east coast. They were brought here either for their own sake or because of what they contained. We do not know what Bedford had to offer in return during these early days.

Saxo-Norman domestic pottery

Much of the trading in markets and shops was by barter and most households would try to be self-sufficient. There would have been no paper bags; pieces of cloth and woven baskets had to do. There were butchers, but live animals and birds would be sold for meat just as they are in some parts of the continent today. Women spun wool and wove cloth, and we have found many of their tools, made from bone or stone. Even bone needles for sewing and bone toggles for fastening clothes have been discovered. Shoes were made from the skins of animals slaughtered for meat. Life was hard, but it had its lighter side too. We know they played games with counters and skated on the river with skates made of horse bones. The Saxons are known to have loved music and storytelling, honeycakes and ale.

Bone skates, 11th or 12th century

6 The Normans and Bedford Castle

After King Harold was killed at the battle of Hastings in 1066, the town of Bedford was seized by the Norman army during its victorious march through England. William the Conqueror made one of his followers, Ralf de Tallebosc, sheriff and castellan, and granted him the lands of the local Saxon thegn (or lord), Anschil of Ware.

The Early Castle

Ralf must have built the earliest castle almost immediately. This would have been a huge and dominating hill of earth with a wooden tower on it. Placed over the eastern boundary of the Saxon town, it had a courtyard to the west, all surrounded by a high fenced bank and ditch.

The Normans needed a safe place from which to overlook the town, defend it against attack, defend themselves against the town, and, if necessary, escape into the countryside. To provide a clear space for the castle and its defence, the Normans must have ruthlessly flattened about a quarter of the Saxon town north of the river, probably using the local people as labour. Houses were razed to the ground and their occupants made homeless.

By 1087, William had granted the barony of Bedford to Hugh de Beauchamp, who had married Ralf's daughter Matilda. The Beauchamp family held the castle with brief interruptions until its end in 1224. During this period the town of Bedford gained a charter confirming its privileges as a borough. The surviving document dates to 1166, but may have been repeating an earlier charter, perhaps by Henry I who reigned from 1100-1135.

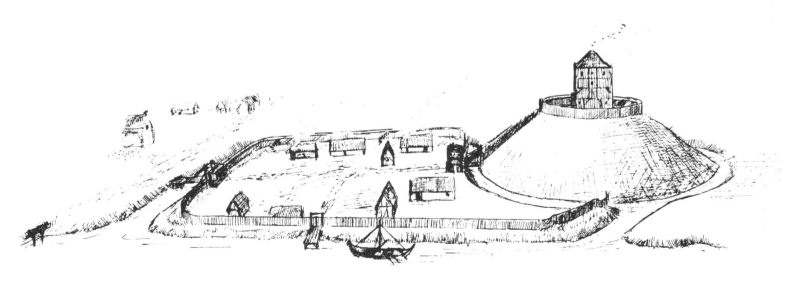

How the early castle might have appeared c.1080. Notice the differences compared with the castle shown in the extract from the reconstructed map of Bedford c.1215-1220 on the opposite page

Expansion and Sieges

At the end of the 11th century, Hugh de Beauchamp may have begun to enlarge the original earth-and-timber castle, replacing it with stone buildings and defences. By the 1130s a chronicler noted there was

a strong and unshakable keep

and a strong high wall. By the early 13th century the fortifications filled most of the area now bounded by the High Street, the Embankment, Newnham Road and Ram Yard. Unfortunately, we know little detail because the Beauchamps repaired the castle themselves and therefore it was rarely mentioned in royal documents.

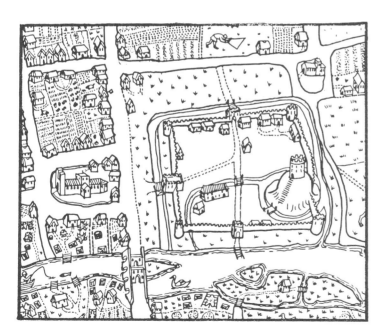

In 1137, during the civil wars, King Stephen tried to take the castle away from the Beauchamp family, and there was a siege. Miles de Beauchamp, grandson of Hugh,

forcibly took from everyone and carried away with him any food on which he could lay hands, and shamelessly robbing the townsmen and their neighbours,

the very people he had previously specially protected as his dependents, and

he gathered in the castle everything that met his eyes.

When his supplies ran out, he gave up the castle, but regained it again in 1141, at the end of the wars.

There were further civil wars. King Stephen's men had control of the castle once again when in 1153 Prince Henry (later King Henry II)

suddenly arrived at the town of Bedford, where the king's supporters had taken refuge in a very strong castle, and, after heavily plundering the town, delivered it to the flames.

St Paul's Church suffered, but we do not know how extensively the town was damaged.

Falkes de Breauté

The next conflict began in 1215 when barons met at Bedford Castle in a minor rebellion against King John. He sent Falkes de Breauté to attack it, and as a result, William de Beauchamp lost his home for nine years. Falkes was a mercenary soldier who had travelled in Europe and knew about the latest developments in fortification and warfare. The chronicler Ralph de Coggeshall recorded that he

strengthened and expanded the castle at great expense, fortifying it with towers and outworks and a variety of warlike machines. He pulled down to the foundations the great church of St Paul which from antiquity had stood next to the castle, and the church of St Cuthbert, and with the stones of the churches he built towers, walls and outer walls, and surrounded it on all sides with deep paved ditches.

Falkes is very definitely portrayed as the local villain. The chronicler, who may have been biased, records that he instructed his men to rape and pillage the local countryside, even attacking church property. His wicked behaviour reached new heights when he refused his just punishment by putting his judges in chains. His original protector, King John, died in 1216; the new young king, Henry III, eventually decided that the law of the land must be upheld, and Falkes punished.

The Final Siege

This was the reason for the famous siege of Bedford Castle in 1224. Falkes himself was wisely absent, and his brother William led resistance to the king's forces. Equipment and supplies were brought in from all over the country, ranging from siege machines like mangonels to quarrel bolts for crossbows. The royal party also required luxuries like spices, wine and even greyhounds for sport.

There was a dramatic struggle lasting two months, recorded by Matthew Paris, chronicler of Dunstable Priory. When it was over, 80 men, including Falkes' brother William and his lieutenants, were hung. The chronicler made a bloodthirsty little sketch of the besieged keep and the executions in the margin of his manuscript. Falkes himself was exiled.

left **a trebuchet and a siege tower**

22

Matthew Paris' Account of the Siege of Bedford Castle

. . . the castle was captured in this way. On the east there was one petrary and two mangonels which attacked the tower every day. On the west side there were two mangonels which battered the old tower. And there was one mangonel on the south and one on the north which made two entrances in the walls nearest them. Besides these there were two wooden towers made by a carpenter raised above the top of the tower and castle for the use of crossbowmen and spies. In addition to these there were several engines in which both crossbowmen and slingers hid in ambush. In addition there was a siege machine called the Cat, beneath which underground diggers called miners could go in and out while they undermined the walls of the tower and castle.

The castle was taken in four assaults. In the first the barbican was captured where four or five outsiders were killed. In the second the outer bailey was captured, where several were killed and our men acquired horses with harness, breastplates, crossbows, oxen, bacon and live pigs and countless other plunder. They burnt the outhouses with the corn and hay which were inside. In the third assault a wall near the old keep fell because of the action of miners and our men entered there and seized the inner bailey in face of great danger. In this occupation many of our men perished. Ten of our men, too, wishing to enter the keep, were shut in and held by the enemy. But at the fourth assault, on the Eve of the Assumption, about the time of Vespers, miners set fire to the keep so that smoke poured into the room in the keep where the enemy were; the keep cracked with the result that fissures appeared in its side. Then since the enemy despaired of their safety, Falkes wife and all the women with her, and Henry, the King's Justiciar, with the other knights who had previously been imprisoned, were allowed to leave safe and sound and the enemy subjected themselves to the King's commands, hoisting his standard at the top of the keep . . .

(Translation by Elizabeth North)

The sketch in the margin of Matthew Paris' Chronicle. We have no way of knowing whether it shows a stylised castle or the real thing.

The king ordered the fortifications to be dismantled. The main tower or keep was to be flattened. The stone-lined ditch that encircled the castle motte was to be filled to the brim. The defences of the outer bailey were to be totally demolished and all the other ditches filled too. The walls of the inner courtyard were to be halved in height, and three of the four ancient towers were to be pulled down. Three-quarters of the ancient tower near St Paul's church was to be removed. Not surprisingly this efficient demolition job finished Bedford Castle as a military stronghold. Never again would it be strong enough to challenge the authority of the crown. William de Beauchamp was allowed to build an unfortified house in the inner courtyard from the stone rubble. He protested in vain that this would not be an impressive enough stronghold for the Baron of Bedford. We have not found William's house, but by 1361 the castle area had become a wasteland used mostly for dumping rubbish, a
void plot of old enclosed by walls.
It remained unoccupied until the 18th or early 19th centuries. The loss of the castle must have been a severe blow to local tradesmen, and the town's biggest employer had vanished overnight.

Foundations of the walltower or watergate excavated on the site of the old County Library

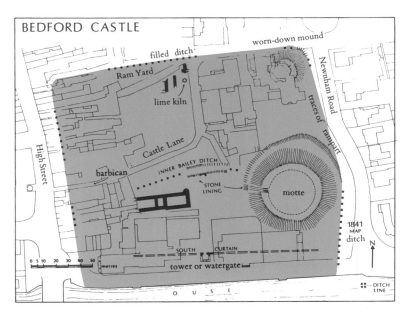

The Limits of the Castle

It is difficult to fit these medieval descriptions with the results of recent archaeological excavations. These discoveries show how little we really know. They have disproved previous modern reconstructions without replacing them with an alternative.

What we have known for some time are the early 13th century limits of the castle at its most powerful. The *west* side was marked by an outer ditch between the Swan Hotel and Ram Yard. This ran to the rear of the buildings facing High Street, but set back a little from the present building line. In the middle, virtually facing St Paul's Church, was the barbican or main entrance, a strongly fortified gateway opening on to an inner roadway. Castle Lane probably preserves this entrance, and the slight bend about 30 metres along it may mark the edge of the outer courtyard.

The Victorians could see the dip of the filled *northern* outer ditch running eastwards for about 200 metres along Ram Yard from High Street. 16th and 18th century property deeds mention it as a boundary obvious enough to define land. There may have been an entrance on the north side, about where Castle Lane meets Ram Yard, and some foundations were found in the recent excavations. At the north-east corner, parts of the Cecil Higgins Art Gallery stand on a worn-down mound of earth, and stonework was found during building in the 1840s. This may have been a defensive tower. The *east* side of the castle was marked by a ditch shown on a map of 1841 running along Newnham Road. There are some traces of a rampart or bank of earth by the remains of the main mound.

The *southern* limit of the castle was the river itself, and there may have been a wall running along the slope down to the water. The remains of a tower or watergate were excavated on the site of the old County Library. This moat was probably water-filled, helped by the natural springs rising from the underlying limestone.

The Motte

The main mound, or 'motte', gives little idea of its former power and strength. The stone tower was destroyed after the siege; the top of the mound was shaved off and pushed over the sides, filling up the ditches. The archaeologists found the ditch had been stone-lined. In the mud at the bottom were several large round stones, mangonel shot, which had bounced off the keep during the siege.

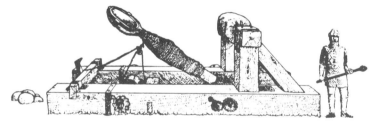

A mangonel: shot like those piled on the left were found in the motte ditch

The Lime Kiln

On the northern edge of the castle was a huge lime kiln. Lime was essential for making the mortar to bond stonework. The kiln was probably in use at the time of Falkes' final improvements. It was nearly 6 metres across at the top, nearly 3 metres deep, and had two stoke holes. It was built into a bank which may have been part of the northern defences. This would have allowed easy access to fill it with limestone or chalk for firing. Some of the last lime made in the kiln was still left in the four air channels at the bottom.

The Lime kiln in Ram Yard

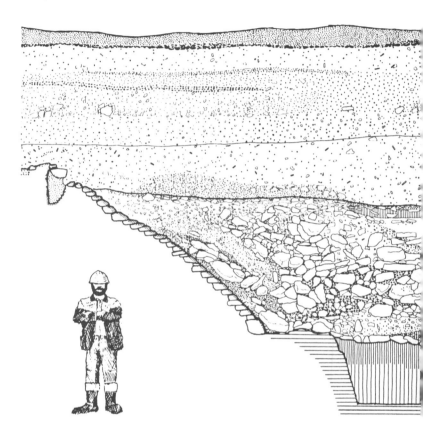

The stone lining for the inner bailey ditch can be seen on the left hand side of the cross-section drawing

The Inner Bailey Ditch

Another completely new discovery made in the recent excavations was a massive stone-lined ditch running west from the mound towards the High Street. This may have been the ditch around the original outer courtyard, later made into the division between outer and inner courtyard when the castle was expanded. The slice dug through this ditch gives an idea of how archaeologists try to reconstruct the past by peeling back the layers of soil accumulating over centuries.

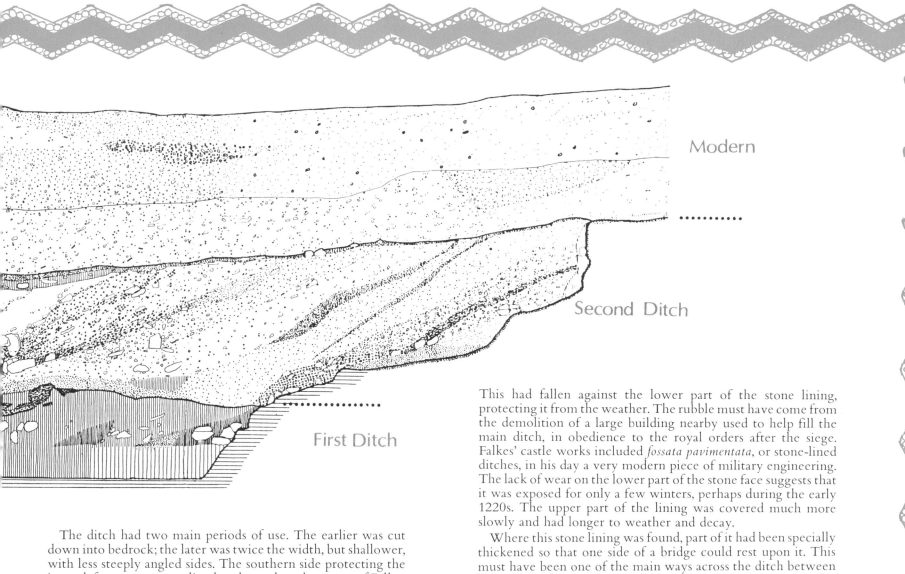

Modern

Second Ditch

First Ditch

This had fallen against the lower part of the stone lining, protecting it from the weather. The rubble must have come from the demolition of a large building nearby used to help fill the main ditch, in obedience to the royal orders after the siege. Falkes' castle works included *fossata pavimentata*, or stone-lined ditches, in his day a very modern piece of military engineering. The lack of wear on the lower part of the stone face suggests that it was exposed for only a few winters, perhaps during the early 1220s. The upper part of the lining was covered much more slowly and had longer to weather and decay.

Where this stone lining was found, part of it had been specially thickened so that one side of a bridge could rest upon it. This must have been one of the main ways across the ditch between the inner and outer courtyards. Cobbling for a roadway was also found leading from it towards the river and the watergate.

The building pushed over to fill up the ditch may have been the one which stood close to its southern side. Its walls were very thick in places, and it had a circular staircase turret at one corner. It had been altered several times, and it may have been part of a range including a hall.

The ditch had two main periods of use. The earlier was cut down into bedrock; the later was twice the width, but shallower, with less steeply angled sides. The southern side protecting the inner defences was stone-lined, and must have been part of Falkes de Breauté's extensive refortification. The upper metre of this stone lining was badly worn, but the lower part was in excellent condition. The original mortar still stood out between the stones, undamaged by frost and wear.

The reason for this difference was easy to see. The ditch had been filled with a mass of rubble tipped over the southern side.

7 Churches and Monasteries

The early Saxon newcomers to the Ouse valley were pagans. Their gods were Woden, Thunor and Tiw. They worshipped them at springs and in sacred groves; one may be marked by the name of Harrowden near Bedford.

Christian missionaries came from the north, following the conversion of a Mercian king in the 7th century. By the 8th century Bedford probably had its earliest St Paul's Church. This was a minster, or the base for several priests serving nearby communities.

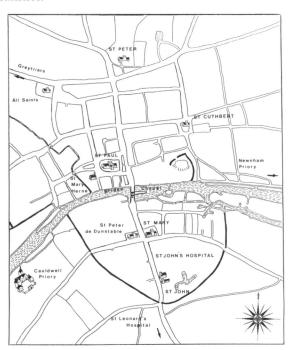

Churches and Monasteries in central Bedford: those surviving today are shown in CAPITALS

Parishes and Churches

Parish boundaries began to be defined during the later part of the Saxon period. The original St Paul's may have been a large regular shaped area around the town north of the river. Later, the rural parishes were laid out up to its boundaries. St Peter's and St Cuthbert's were then carved out of St Paul's, perhaps in the 10th century. Next, after Edward the Elder recaptured the town from the Danes in 915, he may have founded St Mary's to serve his borough south of the river, taking parts from the north ends of Kempston and Elstow parishes.

Other churches were founded just before or after the Normans took over. Religious feeling was strong at these times, and Bedford was expanding beyond the area covered by its early defences. All Saints, at the top of All Hallows, served a small population at the north-west of the town. South of the river, St Peter de Dunstable faced St Mary's. By 1200 there was a chapel on the stone bridge, and the Beauchamps may have had a private chapel in the castle. The chapel of St Mary Herne, which used to stand near the present modern town hall, also existed by 1200.

Monasteries

The Normans came at a time when monasteries were spreading over Europe. About 1153, an Augustinian priory was founded at Cauldwell, just to the south-west of the town. About 1166, one of the group of priests attached to St Paul's Church, Philip de Broy, killed a man, and Simon de Beauchamp moved them out of the town. By 1178 they were living in a brand-new Augustinian priory east of the town at Newnham. In the late 12th century, St John's Hospital was built within St Mary's parish to help the needy poor of Bedford. By 1207, St Leonard's Hospital for lepers stood safely outside the southern limits of the town. The Franciscan friars, dedicated to poverty and preaching, came to Bedford in 1238, and their church near Greyfriars and Priory Street had been built by 1295. In the later middle ages, Bedford, a town of less than 2,000 people, had at least thirteen churches or religious communities.

This changed in the 16th century, and by John Speed's time many of them had gone. Henry VIII dissolved Cauldwell Priory in 1536, the Greyfriars in 1538, and Newnham in 1541. In 1448 the parishes of St Mary and St Peter de Dunstable south of the

THE EAST VIEW OF BEDFORD-PRIORY.

THIS *Priory** was dedicated to S.ᵗ Paul; and was founded before the Norman Conquest, for Canons Secular or Prebendaries: but in the Reign of K: H: I. one of the Canons having kill'd a Butcher in a fray, they were forc'd to remove from thence to a place call'd Newnham; where Roise Wife to Paganus Baron of Bedford built a Priory to receive them.

S. & N. Buck Delin. et Sculp. 1730.

river were united, and in 1546 the church of St Peter de Dunstable was pulled down. The chapel on the old bridge was converted into a gaol in 1589.

Remains of the **Greyfriars** survived near the site of modern Priory School until 1899, when Bedford Corporation had them pulled down. The Buck Brothers engraved a fine set of buildings in the 1730s, but wrongly labelled them as Bedford (i.e. Newnham) Priory.

The engraving *above* has caused much confusion. It shows the remains of the Greyfriars in 1730, but the caption 'Bedford Priory' together with the three lines of text refer to Newnham Priory on the other side of the town.

29

St Paul's Church from the south in 1787

St Peter's Church *c.*1820: how much can you recognise today?

St Paul's Church shows few signs of its long and eventful history. The present building is 15th century with many 19th century alterations, and may be the fifth on the site.

The *first* church was the small minster, perhaps first built in the late 7th or 8th centuries to house the Saxon priests who brought Christianity to the Bedford area. The street grid was laid down around it. The chronicles say Archbishop Oskytel of York was buried there in 956, and it had become a monastery by the early 11th century. This monastery may have been destroyed in the Viking raid of 1009-1010.

The *second* church therefore probably dates from the 11th century. It was seriously damaged or even destroyed in 1153 when Prince Henry besieged King Stephen's men in the castle. Its replacement, the *third* church, was demolished by Fawkes de Breaute to strengthen Bedford Castle, sometime after 1216.

The *fourth* church was built by the citizens of Bedford with stone granted to them from the demolition of the castle after the siege of 1224.

The present church must be the *fifth*, because it contains so little 13th century work. Whatever was rebuilt after the 1220s must have been largely replaced two centuries later, with newer and grander architecture. The Victorians added the north aisle and rebuilt the tower.

Each church was probably larger than the one before it. The foundations of the earlier churches lie under the present one, if they have not been destroyed by later building works or grave digging.

St Peter's Church was drastically enlarged by the Victorians to serve the growing population of 19th century north Bedford. We know this from Thomas Fisher's watercolour of 1820 which shows a late Saxon church altered in the medieval period. The very first church, possibly of timber rather than stone, was probably built in the late 9th or early 10th centuries. The bottom of the present central tower was the west tower of the 11th century church which would have had a chancel to the east. The Normans heightened the tower and added a nave to the west. The Norman door shown in Fisher's watercolour came from St Peter de Dunstable when it was demolished in 1546. The Norman nave was removed in the 19th century when battlements were also added to the top of the tower.

St Mary's is one of the most interesting and complicated churches in Bedford. The original building must have dated from the early 10th century when the southern burh was laid out by Edward the Elder. The present building, the second or third, has stonework in the tower and south transept dating from just before or just after the Norman Conquest. The nave was rebuilt in the 12th century and the chancel in the 14th. A north aisle was added in the 16th century with stone from St Peter de Dunstable, presumably extending the church to include the congregation from the demolished church. The south aisle is Victorian, added to house an expanding 19th century population.

St Mary's Church *c*.1820: the south (right hand) aisle was added later

St Peter de Dunstable was founded in the 11th or 12th centuries, it stood nearby the modern Youth Employment Centre, opposite St Mary's, the original church in the southern burh. Norman south Bedford may have needed two parish churches, but by 1448 they had a single parson. The next hundred years saw rivalry between congregations and an undignified shuttle across St Mary's Street, with the unhappy priest
serving one weeke in one churche and another weeke in another churche, remoovinge everie Saterday from the one to the other, with no little hirte both of the bookes and also of the ornaments.
Demolition was finally agreed in 1546, and the stone was distributed usefully around the town. It built a north aisle for St Mary's Church and helped pave the parish. It also went to repair the Town Bridge. North of the river went doors and a window, to improve the Free School and St Peter's Church. John Williams, that year's Mayor, took enough stone to make a bear-baiting yard in front of his house. Thus the church vanished from sight until the 1970s, when builders trenches found a church wall foundation and parts of 52 skeletons from the parish graveyard.

The **Chapel of St Mary Herne** also was pulled down before cameras had been invented. Watercolours and engravings show a late medieval building, though it existed by 1200. It was owned by the bishop of Lincoln and supported priests at St Paul's Church.　　*(above and below)*

St Cuthbert's Church was also rebuilt several times. St Cuthbert is a Saxon saint's name. An original 10th century timber church may have been replaced in stone by 1200. Around 1216 like the fourth St Paul's, it was raided for castle-building stone by Fawkes de Breauté. The church shown in 18th and early 19th century drawings must be its replacement, rebuilt after the siege. This in turn gave away to the present neo-Norman style building which dates from 1846-47.　　*(above)*

St John's Church began as the private chapel for the nearby hospital, which was founded about 1180. By 1321 it had become the parish church of St John, and the present building shows work mainly of the 14th, 15th and 19th centuries. The hospital building has been renovated to become the headquarters of the St John Ambulance brigade, and is described in more detail later.

All Saints' is the least known of Bedford's medieval churches. It was first mentioned in a document of 1221. Its rectory and churchyard appear in the survey of rents belonging to Newnham Priory in 1506, and it is shown on John Speed's map of 1610. The date of demolition, its exact site and appearance are all unknown, but it may have been a simple chapel-like structure.

St Leonard's Hospital was a home for lepers. There are drawings of the farmhouse which stood there before the railway station was built, but this may not even be medieval, let alone the actual hospital.   *(above)*

The **chapel on the town bridge** existed by the late 12th century. It supported a priest who sought to extract alms from travellers crossing the river by offering to pray for them. In 1331 the townsmen built a second chapel, dedicated to St Thomas. The priest in charge was meant to collect money from travellers to pay for the repair of the bridge. This chapel appears to have fallen into disrepair before the 1530s. The 18th century engravings show both, long after they had ceased to be chapels.

All that survives of **Newnham Priory** are earthworks for fish-ponds near the Marina, and some lengths of wall which are probably the 16th century western boundary. Any remains of the church and cloisters lie under the Bedford Borough's Newnham Avenue Works Depot and the allotments to the east of it.

The site of **Cauldwell Priory** is mentioned in various land deeds, but no pictorial record has survived. Its remains lie mostly under the Britannia Iron Works. Some skeletons from the monks' graveyard were recently found during trenching work.

8 Two Medieval Houses

Only two Bedford buildings other than churches survive from the medieval period. All the other evidence consists of buried foundations, or rubble-filled trenches from which the stone had been robbed for reuse elsewhere. The photo *below* shows typical late medieval foundations discovered during rescue excavations in 1971 next door to the old Angler's Inn in St Mary's Street.

St John's Hospital

This building's history stretches back to the late 12th century. The Hospital was founded by Robert de Parys and John and Henry St John in the 1180s. Its master and brethren were to live in common, observe the daily round of religious services and give charity to the deserving poor of Bedford. The nearby church of St John belonged to them, and seems to have acted as hospital chapel and later as parish church.

The earliest remains in the present buildings may represent a late 12th century open hall at right angles to the street. In the 15th century, it was drastically remodelled: a floor with finely carved woodwork was inserted to make it two-storey. It became quite a comfortable lodging, perhaps for the Master. In 1547, when the Hospitals followed the monasteries into dissolution, it was reported that there were no more brethren and that

there is found never a poor person nor hath not been by the space of many years.

However, the Hospital building survived: it was altered further in the 17th century by which time it had become the Rectory House. It was restored in 1969-70.

St John's Hospital *c.*1820: the tower of the separate church is beyond

The Old George

Behind Debenhams in the High Street, and reached from an alley running between St Paul's Square and Silver Street, stand the fragmentary remains of the Old George Inn. Documents mention it in the 15th century. Drawings and photographs, made before piecemeal demolition after 1937, show late medieval details.

The Prior of Newnham owned the land in the 15th century, and this has given rise to the tale that the Old George was his town house: more likely it was an inn. The longest surviving part runs parallel to High Street, and formed the west side of the courtyard, entered through an arch in its middle. Dudley Cary Elwes, a Victorian antiquary, described some of the decoration: *on each side of the arch facing the High Street are two niches with shields; the right is a cross of St George; the left is an old coat of arms of the town. Over the right niche and above the string course is a niche with a figure of George and the Dragon.*

Compare the engraving by Bradford Rudge, made over a century ago, with what can be seen today on the inside of the courtyard. Little survives and most of the range has been completely rebuilt, though some details can still be seen at ground floor level.

The inner face of the Old George Yard, as seen by Bradford Rudge in the mid 19th century, and today. A few details still survive despite the major alterations.

9 Life in Norman and Medieval Bedford

In the 13th century the population of the town may have been less than 2,000, compared with today's total of 73,500. Even so, Bedford was the county town and the market centre for the surrounding countryside. By 1297 no fewer than 10 village names are reflected in the surnames of Bedford's richest burghers. Some of their ancestors may have been serfs who had gained freedom from their feudal lords by staying in Bedford for a year and a day without being caught.

Wealth and Poverty

We can guess how many people lived in Bedford from a document of 1297 recording the townsfolks' taxable property. This tells us there were 98 Bedfordians with enough property to tax. 51 owned belongings worth less than £1, and they were the wealthy men. Many more families had far less, and perhaps 300 households were too poor to be recorded. These people lived in conditions not so different from the poverty often found in the Third World. Houses were not like those picturesque cottages in today's villages, built centuries after this time and then for wealthier folk. The 13th century poor had single roomed thatched cottages too flimsy to last more than a few decades, but there were some stone and tiled houses in medieval Bedford. Heating and cooking was much like the earlier periods, but prepared food like pies or bread could be carried to a professional baker to cook in ovens like the ones found in St Mary's Street.

left **an oven reconstructed**

The base of a medieval oven found in St Mary's Street.

Mill Street

14th century floor tiles

15th century knight roof finial

Medieval painted glass found in St Mary's Street

Water, Drainage and Rubbish

Running down to the river in the north-west part of the town was the Saffron Ditch, crossed by small bridges where roads ran across it. In the days without sewage systems, such ditches were used to carry away effluents and rubbish. There was no waste disposal service. Rubbish was also spread over the fields as manure, thrown into the river, or buried in pits dug into back gardens. Most of these pits were used as cess-pits, where chamber pots were emptied. Typical of the pattern of pits and building traces is this complicated excavation in St John's Street.

Water drainage and water supplies were very important to the townsfolk. The southern part of the town had a tendency to flood. Ditches were dug both as boundary markers and as drainage channels. Public water supplies were wells in streets, though many houses would have had their own. A particularly fine example was found in St John's Street; it had a flight of steps leading down into it, and a wooden building over it to keep the water clean. Rather less water was used for cooking and cleaning than we consume today. Carrying heavy buckets of water was a great deterrent to wasteful use.

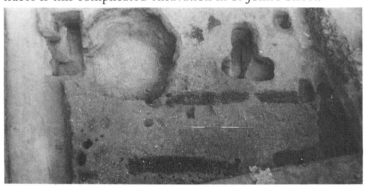

Pits in St John's Street

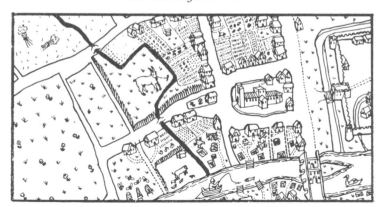

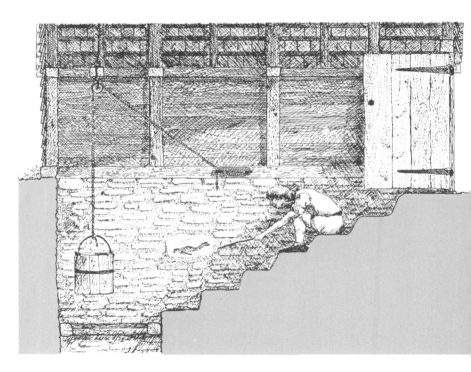

Reconstruction of well house found in St John's Street

Musical instruments: whistle, tuning peg, fipple flute and (post-medieval) jews harp *(right)*

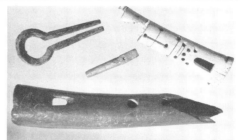

The contents of rubbish pits show what people were cultivating and what was in their natural environment. The meadows were full of flowers; the mixed hedges grown to keep animals in check contained varieties such as blackthorn, hawthorn, hazel and dogwood. Sloes and wild fruit, seeds and herbs for medicine have also been found in pits. Some of the fruit doubtless found its way into country wines, served in the grander homes from shiny green glazed jugs like this one which came originally from the Oxford area.

Games and Leisure

Hunting and hawking were favourite Norman activities, and arrow heads and bells from falcons' jesses (or strings) have been found. People had to make their own entertainment. Waking hours were closely matched by daylight hours in the days when only candles and firelight were available after the sun had set. Winter evenings were whiled away with stories and music. We have found the copper fixtures from manuscript books which were rare and precious in the days before printing. Music played an important part, and small fragments of musical instruments have survived. Although the wood has long since rotted away, some of the ivory pegs from stringed instruments have been found, still showing the green staining from their copper ended strings. Deep in the moat surrounding the castle motte was the remains of a flute carved out from an animal bone.

Gambling was a favourite pastime of some; gaming counters and dice have been found. Chess too was played. Other, less pleasant, sports like bull-baiting are known to have been popular, but traces are more difficult to find.

13th century jug from the Oxford area

An Impression of early 13th century Bedford

This map (also on the back and front covers) tries to show the town as it might have looked about 1215-1220. Bedford's grid plan made it easy to divide the land into plots. Each cottage had its own piece of land, many with gardens full of crops and fruit trees. Each household could grow much of its own vegetables and fruit, keep chickens perhaps, and hives full of bees which provided honey for sweetening food and drink. You can see a cow being milked and a goat tethered by the Saffron Ditch. Sheep too would be milked to provide delicious cheese and cream. Look closely and you will see pigs. Up to the present century, in country areas, the villagers kept pigs in back gardens. They provided dung to fertilise the garden, lard for cooking, greasing machinery and making ointments. Their bones are commonly found in excavations in the town. Pigs provide fresh meat and offal in return for eating waste food, as well as giving smoked sausages, bacon or salt pork to last the long hard winter. People in St John's Street showed a marked preference for beef.

Bones show marks from butchers knives made hundreds of years ago. We know that Bedford people kept both guard dogs and pet dogs from the skeletons we have found, and dog teeth marks gnawed into old bones. Only the Castle folk appeared to be eating venison, and this probably reflected the strict hunting laws. We don't find rabbits before the Norman period, but throughout the Middle Ages people ate a great variety of birds and beasts including many wild birds.

Medieval dog burials in Cauldwell Street

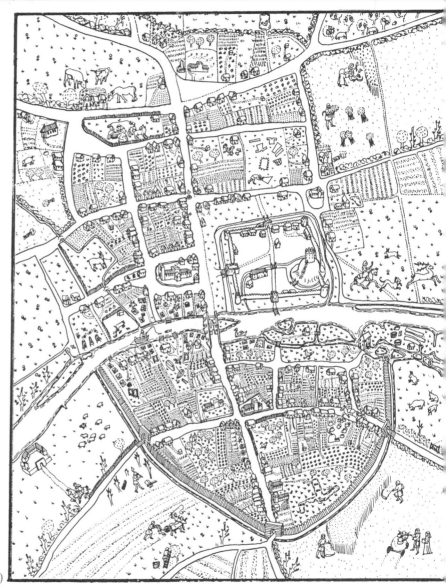

Trade and Industry

Bedford in the Middle Ages was for all practical purposes two towns, one on either side of the river. The people were even taxed separately as the 'Men of Bedford' (north) and the 'Men beyond the bridge of Bedford' (south). Trading patterns were slightly different north and south of the river, with people looking to different areas for buying and selling.

Many more pots were used in the medieval period, and trading was more widespread, helping us to see where the Bedford people of the day were buying and selling. Bedford had its own pottery industry. We know there was a potter in the town in the year 1297; later on, Cardington Road was called Potter Street. Throughout the town locally made pieces of pottery have been found but we have yet to unearth the workshop.

Seal of Ralph de Torfreville, a Norman. Lost in Bedford Castle around 1200.

The river has always played an important part in the life of Bedford. It was a route for trade and travel, and a source of food. In 1297 Bedford had a merchant selling sea-coal, and its own fisherman. The River must have been better stocked with fish, even though the stretch that ran through the town was probably foul with rubbish and sewage.

Various documents mention smiths and a goldsmith: archaeology has shown smelting of iron, silver and copper in Midland Road. Bedford Castle had a lime kiln in the 13th century; there was a 14th century lime burner called Simon, and John Speed's map of 1610 shows a lime kiln off Lime Street.

Medieval flask or bottle

41

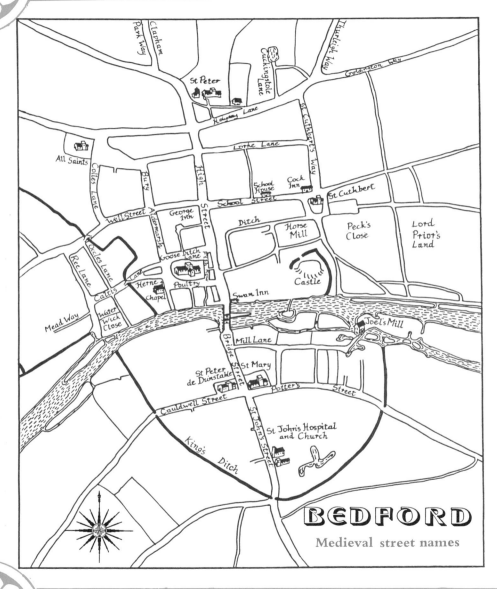

BEDFORD

Medieval street names

There were many more little streets, lanes and alleyways than there are today. South of St Paul's Church, three lanes led down to the river's edge. The one nearest the bridge was called Little Lane, and the middle one, Pudding Lane. Some of these names have survived from 1297, others occur in another document of 1506-7. South of St Paul's Church was the Poultry Market; the Meat Market was to the north. The fish sellers were in Fish Row. The Market, marked by a stone cross, was held at the cross-roads where the High Street meets Mill Street and Silver Street, then called Gaol Lane because the County Gaol stood on the corner. All these existed about 1500, but many were earlier. The Town Bridge shown is the old one. The modern bridge is placed slightly to the east, and the High Street now curves slightly to meet it.

Inside the town the Castle dominated. The great courtyards or baileys were crammed with buildings. Nowadays the deep wide ditch to the west is covered by High Street shops, and the present road runs where the grass verge is shown. Opposite the main castle entrance – or barbican – was old St Paul's Church, the building later pulled down by Falkes de Breauté for building stone. Castle Lane today still winds its way into the Castle area. For most of the townsfolk the castle must have been at least partly welcomed as a source of income and employment as well as a stimulus for trade.

A selection of medieval buckles and brooches excavated in Bedford

The town boasted no fewer than 11 tanners along its river banks, many of them on the north side. Maybe they used oak bark from the trees along the road to Goldington. The other ingredients for tanning skins when they had been scraped clean of rotting flesh were urine and excreta. Skins had to soak for many days in stinking pits. Perhaps it was not a very pleasant trade, but it was a highly profitable one. John by the Wall was a farmer-cum-tanner, and was by far Bedford's richest inhabitant at the end of the 13th century.

Leather shoe soles

Evidence of a horn industry has been found in St John's Street and Midland Road, probably supplying the town with spoons and drinking cups. Also in St John's Street, hundreds of bones from horses were found, perhaps indicating stables conveniently placed near the main route through the town. Documents tell us of shoemakers, and scraps of waterlogged shoes have been found in excavations. The dyer left his mark in the name Fuller Street, though we no longer know where this was. Other tradesmen, recorded in 1297 included general merchants, a saltseller, a spicer, a rope maker and carpenter; there were wheelwrights, a carter, a blanket-maker and dealers in woollen cloth. Like most medieval towns, Bedford could supply most of the necessities and some of the luxuries of life during the medieval period.

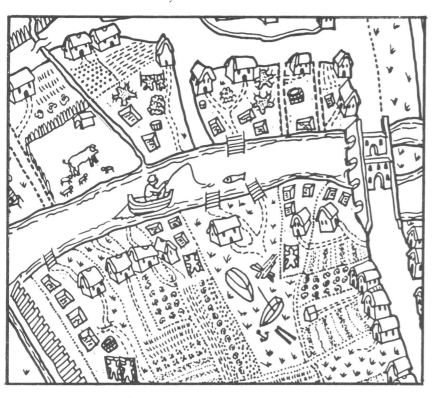

Tanning west of the bridge

Dyers, perhaps by Duck Mill

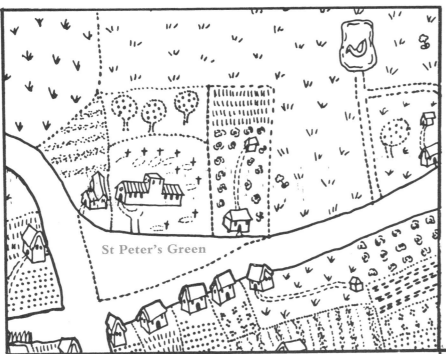

St Peter's Green

Grain drying kiln excavated in St John's Street

Town and Country

Now look to the edge of the map where town and country life merge together. Immediately outside the town limits the open fields and meadows began. Even rich merchants and tradesmen farmed and kept livestock as well as carried on their businesses. Some of the townsfolk can be seen tending beasts in the meadows or letting pigs root around in nearby woodland. Corn and wheat grew on longer stalks than it does today. Men and women cut it by hand with sickles and gathered it into stooks or bundles to dry. Later, when it had been threshed, sacks were taken to one of the watermills on the river to ground grain into flour. The road to the main mill still carries the name of the latest mill, Duck Mill Lane.

Hay was cut by scythe and piled on to carts ready to make into haystacks to provide bedding and fodder for the winter to come. Ploughing was done by pairs of oxen. The woodsmen cut fuel for the winter and apples were picked for storage or cider. On the roads a pack animal laden with goods is led into the town. A baggage seal from such a load is shown on p41. Outside to the west, a monk makes his way to Cauldwell Priory. Safely outside the town is St Leonard's, a hospital for lepers. Also outside the old town limits lies the late Saxon church of St Peter with its green. The neighbouring property is a substantial medieval house called the Bury. The 1506 document tells of Cuckingstole Lane which led up to a pool where nagging wives were ducked for punishment. The late Saxon church of St Cuthbert's lay to the east, with alongside it another property called Peck's House. All Hallows Church lay outside the town to the west. All three churches had settlements around them; Bedford was beginning to grow outside the town walls, though it was still very small by the time John Speed drew his map in the early seventeenth century.

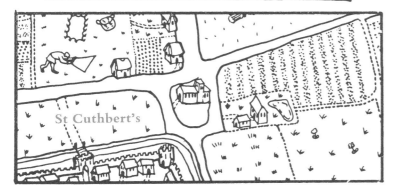

St Cuthbert's

10 How to find out more about Early Bedford

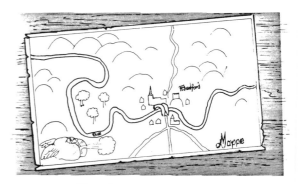

In this booklet we have tried to describe the beginnings of Bedford. There are many gaps in the story, and plenty of uncertainties. The picture we have presented is an outline sketch. What have been the main sources, and where can more be found out?

One of the most important is **map evidence.** No more old maps of Bedford like Speed's will be discovered, but there is plenty to see in those we already have. The detail in Speed's map is fascinating. Reynold's map of 1841, drawn more accurately, shows Bedford when it was just beginning to expand in the 19th century. You can compare what they show with what exists in Bedford today. Copies of these two maps can be bought at the County Record Office, County Hall, Bedford.

Documents are a very important source for early Bedford. Few early manuscripts have survived for present day historians to study. Those we have were written in Old English or a kind of shorthand Latin, and the handwriting is often difficult. Some have been translated and published in the volumes of the *Bedfordshire Historic Record Society,* but they usually still need interpretation by someone familiar with the historical period. They were written for medieval reasons, not to answer our modern questions. Many of these documents are kept in the County Record Office, and the printed records are in the Local History Library in County Hall.

Recently **published historical accounts** of Bedford are based on those documents and should answer many people's questions. The *Bedfordshire Bibliography* has several sections listing these books. Some of the older ones do not include the results of recent work on the development of the town plan and archaeology. The best general books are Joyce Godber's *Story of Bedford* and *History of Bedfordshire.* C. F. Farrar's *Old Bedford,* recently reprinted, is romantic and attractive reading, but often misleading.

Archaeology is a major source of information for the early development of Bedford. It includes studies of how the plan of the town has developed, and the results of actual excavations. One of the aims of this booklet is to summarise the academic articles and technical reports produced by this kind of research. The *Bedfordshire Archaeological Journal,* now *Bedfordshire Archaeology,* reports the results of rescue excavations in the town from 1967, and contains articles on the development of the town plan of Bedford. The actual finds from these excavations are kept in Bedford Museum and a selection is displayed, including some of the objects shown in this booklet.

Further Reading

Bedfordshire Bibliography (published by Bedfordshire Historic Records Society in 4 volumes, 1962, 1967, 1971, 1978). A comprehensive reference work.

Victoria County History of Bedfordshire, 3, 1912, 1-33. A little outdated and selective, but a useful scholarly summary.

Joyce Godber, *The History of Bedfordshire,* 1969. The standard county history, with plenty of material about Bedford put in a county and wider context.

D. H. Hill, Late Saxon Bedford, *Bedfordshire Archaeological Journal* 5 1970, 96-99. The theory that the town north of the river was planned by Edward the Elder in 915-916.

Joyce Godber, *The Story of Bedford,* 1978. A selective expansion of material on Bedford from her History of Bedfordshire.

Jane Hassall and David Baker, Bedford: Aspects of Town Origins and Development, *Bedfordshire Archaeological Journal* 9 1974 74-94. The predecessor of this booklet, though it goes beyond 1600; it repeats the 'Hill' theory of town origins.

David Baker, Evelyn Baker, Jane Hassall and Angela Simco, Excavations in Bedford 1967-77, *Bedfordshire Archaeological Journal* 13 1979. The full published report for most of the rescue excavations in Bedford. It also summarises both theories of town origins north of the river.

Jeremy Haslam, The Origin and Plan of Bedford, *Bedfordshire Archaeology* 16 1983, 29-36. Outlines the theory that Offa was the planner of the town north of the river at the end of the 8th century.

Jeremy Haslam, The Ecclesiastical Topography of Medieval Bedford, *Bedfordshire Archaeology,* forthcoming. Expands further the ideas in the previous article and makes suggestions about the development of parishes in Bedford.

Piece of 13th century jug with face decoration

Acknowledgements

This booklet draws upon the sources listed in the section on **Further Reading.** In putting flesh on a small number of surviving historical bones we have inevitably made a number of assumptions which cannot be proved now, or may be disproved later: we hope that these will be sufficiently clear to the reader. Errors have been minimised by the advice of Patricia Bell and Alan Cox, though we are entirely responsible for those that remain. We are particularly grateful to Jeremy Haslam for permission to incorporate material from his current researches and projected articles on the development of early towns in England.

The rescue excavations were conducted by the County Planning Department's Archaeological Field Team, and by others, all in conjunction with Bedford Museum (North Bedfordshire Borough Council): John Turner and Penny Spencer helpfully commented on a draft of this booklet.

The excavations were funded by the County Council, North Bedfordshire Borough Council, the Department of the Environment (now English Heritage), the Manpower Services Commission, and were also supported by the Bedford Archaeological Society and several developers.

The cartoons and reconstructions are by Andrew Pinder. The figures on pages 2 and 3 (by Evelyn Baker) are based on archaeological and manuscript evidence.

Photographs are by Ken Whitbread and Dave Stubbs (Bedfordshire County Council Photographic Unit) – 13, 19, 25, 39, 41, 42, 47; David Baker 15, 24, 26, 34, 35, 37, 38, 40, 44; Verulamium Museum 48.

Watercolours in Chapters 7 and 8 by Thomas Fisher.

The booklet was designed by the authors.